THEOSOPHY
AND
CHRISTIANITY

Theosophical Manual No. XII

Theosophy and Christianity

By

HENRY TRAVERS EDGE

POINT LOMA PUBLICATIONS, INC.
P. O. Box 9966
SAN DIEGO, CALIFORNIA, U.S.A. 92109

ISBN: 0-913004-17

Printed in the United States of America by
Stockton Trade Press, Inc.
Santa Fe Springs, California

CONTENTS

EDITORS' PREFACE

Nature exists and Man exists, and somewhere, unobscured by man's own sophistries there must be available the wisdom and learning which tells us *why* and *how*. As we ponder the question it seems an inevitable conclusion that somewhere there must be preserved a recording, a gathering of facts or 'laws', a formulation in human language of the truth concerning Man and Nature. There must be a basic source from which sciences, philosophies and great religions have sprung.

H. P. Blavatsky, in her writings of immense intellectual and spiritual power — still not fully appreciated — points to that living Source, declaring it exists. She called it the Ancient Wisdom, the Sacred Science, the *Gupta-Vidyâ,* and gave to it the Greek name of *Theosophia,* Theosophy, knowledge and wisdom such as the gods or divinities live by. This Ancient Wisdom, she affirmed, has always been in existence, though not always publicly known, having come down the ages tested and checked by generations of Great Seers. It may be called the Facts of Being, the 'laws' or workings of Nature.

In this series of twelve Theosophical Manuals this Ancient Wisdom in its fundamentals is explained with clarity of presentation and logical appeal by students and scholars who have devoted a lifetime to theosophic study. Above all they have been governed by strict honesty and adherence to the teachings as originally reported and recorded.

The first booklet, *Theosophy: A General View of Occult Doctrine,* outlines the overall teachings, presenting a general picture. Succeeding booklets cover in greater detail the subjects of Reincarnation, Karma, The Seven Principles of Man, Death and the After-Death States of Consciousness, Evolution, Man's Divine Parentage: the Origin of Man and of the Earth, the Doctrine of Cycles, The Ladder of Life: Hierarchies, The Astral Light, Psychic Powers, and Theosophy and Christianity.

It is hoped that these Studies will be received with an open mind, for in them the earnest searcher will find keys that are indispensable to an understanding of the Universe and of Man.

Helen Todd
W. Emmett Small

I

INTRODUCTORY

T HEOSOPHY is the essential truth underlying all religions, and does not recognize any one religion as being supreme over the others or as the last word of truth. It is not hostile to Christianity, but finds itself obliged to combat many things which it considers alien to the genuine Christian gospel and which have gradualy crept in since that gospel was originally proclaimed. Among these is the idea that Christianity is paramount among religions or that it is a final revelation of divine truth, superseding other faiths. This idea is contrary to the truth and is becoming more and more difficult to maintain. For this there are two principal reasons. Ancient religions have been widely and intensively studied, especially those of India, which have become accessible through the knowledge of Sanskirt. Intercommunication between nations has grown so wide and intimate. These two causes combine to prevent the exclusive attitude of the mind which was possible in past times. But it is hard to give up cherished habits, and moreover people imagine that if they surrender the paramoun-

cy of Christianity they will be surrender-
ing religion itself. And so we find strange ex-
pedients resorted to in the attempt to account
for the existence in more ancient religions of
so many of the doctrines and rituals which
were supposed to be peculiar to Christianity.
The Abbé Huc, in his celebrated *Travels in
Tartary, Tibet, and China,* describes how he
found among the Tibetan priests not only
many characteristic doctrines of the Roman
Church but even many of their rituals, ves-
tures, and sacred implements. His explanation is that the Devil thus anticipated Christianity in order to deceive mankind; to which
he adds a theory that early Christian mission-
aries may have penetrated to Tibet. A recent
improvement on this is found in a theory
which we have just seen in a book published
under the auspices of a well-known Christian
propagation society, to the effect that the
lofty doctrines found in India's sacred books
were due to the work of the Holy Spirit, who
thus prepared mankind for the 'greater things
than these' to come in the future. But still it
rests with him to show that the Christianity
which came was really greater.

There are various brands of broad-church
Christianity, which seek to enlarge the scope
of the religions so as to take in many things
now known to man but which did not occupy the minds of our forefathers; but the
difficulty with them is to enlarge the gospel
sufficiently without destroying its identity as

Christianity; and again, if a body of water be widened without increasing its volume, the result is to make it shallower.

At the Church Congress some years ago, the Very Rev. W. R. Matthews, Dean of St. Paul's Cathedral, London, said that until recently almost the whole of Christendom would have said that there is one revelation of God, and that it is to be found in the Bible; but (he continued) the supreme revelation is not wholly external and we cannot recognize the 'Word made Flesh' unless the Word is within us. He went on to say:

> God does not dictate from heaven a creed or articles of faith. He manifests Himself through the experience and personalities of His prophets and of His Son. The doctrines of the Church are formulas in which the revelation has been summed up, guarded and preserved. . . . It may be that more adequate expressions will be found hereafter for the spiritual heritage that they have been formed to express. . . . The Holy Spirit will guide us into new truth.

When such eminent and leading authorities concede so much, we can hardly be accused of being altogether unorthodox; we are merely pointing out some of the logical conclusions to which the Dean's admissions inevitably point.

These various attempts all tend to the confession that religions change with the times, that humanity progresses independently of them, and that they must keep up with the needs of humanity or else become a drag upon progress. Yet we cannot on this account reject all religious truth and lapse into one of the forms of unbelief, atheism, or materialism. We must not throw away the substance with the outgrown form. An organized religious system, with its creed, its prescribed ritual, its church organization, is a spirit imbodied in a form; and like every other organism, the form has to undergo continual change, though the spirit within may ever be the same. These are facts which cannot be disputed by anyone with a modicum of historical knowledge or an acquaintance with the general laws of growth and evolution.

But there can be only one Truth. Religion itself, apart from creeds and churches, is a recognition and observance of the basic laws of the universe. These basic laws are also inherent in man himself, so that the real eternal and universal Religion is based on the facts of human nature and must remain the same as long as man is man. The most essential truth is that man is a divine spirit incarnate in an animal body; that his salvation consists in subduing his lower nature by means of his higher; and that the true law of conduct for man is that which is expressed in the Golden Rule. This truth lies at the base of all religions, and Christianity, so far from having originated it, or even improved it, has merely inherited it.

It is necessary to refer briefly to certain

Theosophical teachings which will be found more fully treated in other studies, and one of these is the teaching as to the Wisdom-Religion or Secret Doctrine. This is Knowledge concerning the deepest mysteries of nature and man, but in the present cycle of human evolution it is unknown to mankind in general. During this cycle therefore it rests under the guardianship of the Masters of Wisdom, or the Great Lodge of Initiates, whose fuction it is to preserve the sacred knowledge and to communicate it to the world at appropriate times and in appropriate places. They accomplish this work in several ways: one is by sending out a Messenger from themselves, who appears among men, gathers around him a body of disciples, founds an esoteric school in which he gives private instruction, and also gives exoteric teaching to the multitude.* But after the withdrawal of the Teacher, the movement which he has started undergoes changes and degeneration. It falls under the influence of worldly motives and forces; it becomes form-

---

*"And he said, Unto you it is given to know the mysteries of the kingdom of God: but to others in parables; that seeing they might not see, and hearing they might not understand."—*Luke*, viii, 10

"And with many such parables spake he the word unto them [the people], as they were able to hear it. But without a parable spake he not unto them: and when they were alone, he expounded all things to his disciples."—*Mark*, iv, 33-4

alized; it breaks up into schools and sects; it acquires various organic forms with churches, priesthood, and creeds. The process can be traced in the history of religions in general; it can be traced in Christianity, so that the Christianity of today is not in any of its forms the original gospel as given by the founder.

It will be well to say a few words about the attitude towards Christians which we here adopt. That attitude will be sympathetic, and not merely from feeling but from knowledge. For the writer, having been brought up in the Church of England, in an atmosphere more genial than that of some of the narrower sects, and having in early life been a sincere Christian, is thereby qualified to speak with more sympathy and understanding than is sometimes the case with those who can view Christianity only from the outside. Moreover, there will not be the same likelihood of falling into the common forensic error of misrepresenting the case of one's opponent in a controversy, of comparing what is best in Theosophy with what is worst in Christianity, or of attacking men of straw or flogging dead horses.

There is no wish to disturb the peace of those who find in Christianity, as they know it, all they need, and especially those who find in their faith the inspiration to a noble life. But there is a large and increasing number to whom our message may be welcome. The churches confess that they are losing their hold, and there are more people than ever who find themselves unable to accept what they are taught, and who yet cannot throw over religion itself and lapse into infidelity. Such people are at a loss for an expedient; they may find some way of their own, or they may form movements; but in any case their efforts lack both definiteness and co-operation. These needs are supplied by Theosophy; Theosophy comes to the rescue and can justly claim to stand as a champion of Christianity by pointing to the true and original excellence of that religion and showing how to extract the essence from the extraneous matter that encumbers it.

We shall show, then, what are the essential truths of religion, which change not with the times, cause no conflict between creeds and sects, and are enshrined in the heart of man; and we shall trace these in Christianity, its doctrines, its forms, and its scriptures. Thereby we shall prove that Christianity is kin to the other great religions and to the greatest philosophical systems, and that there is enough external evidence to prove that it is one of the effluents of the great river of the Wisdom-Religion. We shall try to trace Christianity from its beginnings, through various changes, to its present forms, so far as that may be possible with imperfect knowledge and in a limited scope. The principal dogmas, articles of faith, and ritual observances must be considered, their real meaning shown by comparison with the corresponding elements in other religons, in philosophies, and in mythologies. It will be shown how the teachings ascribed to Jesus in the Gospels, as well as some of those of his apostles in the Epistles, appear in a new light as soon as we have the key to their interpretation; and how many of such teachings have remained obscure because we had not that key.

Various movements have been started, and exist today, for uniting the world's religions in common service, so that they may pool their efforts instead of contending with each other; and though such efforts are worthy of all praise and have achieved beneficial results, yet their shortcomings and the reasons therefor will be clear in the light of what we are saying. Religions are one in essence, and different in external form. The real way to unite them is to get back to the essence in each; attempts to bring about articial union in externals are not so practicable. Moreover such attempts at unification are apt to take the form of eliminating from the common program the points of difference, so that what remains is a residue more or less vague and lifeless. Such a process resembles subtraction rather than addition; or, better, it is the attempt to find a common factor, which, as we know, becomes smaller in proportion to the multitude of the numbers whose common factor is to be found.

All religions have an esoteric basis beneath their exoteric form, and it is this which has so largely disappeared. Religions as they are do not satisfy the needs of human aspiration, for they leave out so large a part of what vitally concerns man. They are confined chiefly to ethical principles, but tell us nothing about the nature of the universe or the nature of man. Falling thus behind the age, they have allowed to grow up competing influences, such as natural science and abstract philosophy; and so we find the field of knowledge, which should be one, divided into compartments, either independent of each other or else conflicting.

The false antithesis between morals and knowledge, religion and science, righteousness and culture, has been one of the great banes of religion. A unification of the field of knowledge is much desired; a uniform law by which to live; a solid basis for ethics, morals, conduct, instead of dogmas which we cannot believe, or speculations and fads and cults innumerable. A man's real religion is what he lives by—whatever he may profess. Thus the real unification of religions is found, not by trying to force an external union, or by eliminating from them all points of difference and thus leaving a weak residue, but by getting back to the esoteric basis of religions and showing the common parentage of them all; in short, by reviving a knowledge of the ancient Wisdom-Religion.

II

HISTORICAL SKETCH

'PAGAN' ORIGIN OF CHISTIANITY

IN this section we give evidence to show that Christianity was not new, but derived from what went before; that its cardinal doctrines are held in common with older religions; and that many of its rites and dogmas are adopted from what is called Pagan belief. There are people called Fundamentalists, who seek to go back to the true old gospel; but how far back do they propose to go, and just what point in history do they stop at? Let us take a few quotations from early writers on Christianity.

St. Augustine says:

The very thing which is now called the Christian religion, really was known to the ancients, nor was it wanting at any time from the beginning of the human race up to the time Christ came in the flesh; from which time the true religion, which has previously existed, began to be called Christian, and this in our days is the Christian religion, not as having been wanting in former times, but as having in later times received that name.

—*Augustini Opera*, I, 12

Eusebius, another Father, though an ardent

advocate of the new faith, is constrained to admit that the Christian religion was neither new nor strange, and that it was known to the ancients. (*Ecclesiastical History,* see Bk. i, ch. iv.)

Justin Martyr, in defending Christianity before the Emperor Hadrian, is at pains to show its identity with Paganism.

By declaring the Word (*Logos*), the first begotten of God, our Master Jesus Christ, to be born of a virgin without any human mixture, to be crucified and dead and afterwards to have risen and ascended into heaven, we say no more than what you say of those whom you call the sons of Jupiter . . . . As to the objection of our Jesus being crucified, I say that suffering was common to all the afore-mentioned sons of Jupiter, only they suffered another kind of death. . . . As to his curing the lame and the paralytic and such as were cripples from birth, this is little more than what you say of your Aesculapius.—*Apology,* I, chs xxi, xxii

Ammonius Saccas says:

Christianity and Paganism, when rightly understood, differ in no essential points, but had a common origin, and are really one and the same thing.

The following quotation from the controversy between H. P. Blavatsky and the Abbé Roca, published in the French magazine *Le Lotus,* April 1888, [See also *Blavatsky, Collected Writings,* IX p. 224.] is appropriate here:
Writings, IX p. 224.] is appropriate here:

For me, Jesus Christ, that is to say the Man-God of the Christians, a copy of the Avatars of all countries, from the Hindu Krishna as well as the Egyptian

Horus, was never a historical person. He is a deified personification of the glorified type of the great Hierophants of the Temples, and his story told in the New Testament is an allegory, assuredly containing profound esoteric truths, but an allegory. . . . The legend of which I speak is founded . . . on the existence of a personage called Jehoshua (from which 'Jesus' has been made) born at Lud or Lydda about 120 years before the modern era. . . . In spite of all the desperate researches made during long centuries if we place on one side the witness of the 'Evangelists,' i. e., unknown men whose identity has never been established, and that of the *Fathers* of the Church, interested fanatics, neither history nor profane tradition, nor official documents, nor the contemporaries of the *soi-disant* drama, are able to provide one single serious proof of the historical and real existence, not only of the Man-God but even of him called Jesus of Nazareth, from the year 1 to the year 33. All is darkness and silence. Philo Judaeus, born before the Christian era . . . made several journeys to Jerusalem. He went there to write the history of the religious sects of his epoch in Palestine. No writer is more correct in his descriptions, more careful to omit nothing; no community, no fraternity, even the most insignificant, escaped him. Why then does he not speak of the Nazarenes? Why does he not make the most distant allusion to the Apostles, to the divine Galilean, to the Crucifixion? The answer is easy. Because the biography of Jesus was invented after the first century, and no one in Jerusalem was a bit better informed than Philo himself.

These passages, which are only a sample out of what might be adduced, show that Christianity was recognized as being a continuance of an age-old doctrine, with changes in external form made necessary by changing times.

The history of Christianity proves it to
have been inspired by enormous force, all-
conquering vitality, enabling it to last through
the centuries and dominate so much of the
world. And yet, if we seek the origin, we can
find only the most meager foundation. The
historicity of Jesus is very doubtful; his mis-
sion, as recorded in the Gospels, is limited to
a few months and is ignored by Pagan his-
torians. Christianity was a revival of the
Wisdom-Religion, started by some great Messenger from the Lodge, of whom the record
has been lost. The figure in the Gospels is
historically fictitious, but should be considered
as a type-figure of a great Teacher. Such a
Teacher, Theosophy states, did live though
there is little or no factual record of his life.
The Gospels were not written until long after
the time of which they profess to treat; and
Paul in his Epistles seems to know nothing
of them.

There is a Jewish account of a certain
Syrian, named Jeshua or Jehoshua ben Pan-
thera, who lived in the reign of the Jewish
king Alexander Jannaeus about a century
B.C.; and some think the name Jesus was
derived from this. From this man were derived the doctrines of two sects of Jewish
Christians, living before the Christian era,
the Ebionites and the Nazarenes. They represent the purest form of Christianity, and
taught that Christ is in all men, and the doctrines of Aeons or Divine Emanations, where-

by man himself is shown to be a descendant from the highest divinities. Such too was the teaching of the Christian Gnostics and of the Neo-Platonists.

Evidently Christianity was originally a form of the Wisdom-Religion and taught that man is essentially a divine being, the Christ being simply the Divine Spirit in man; and that man must achieve his own salvation by recognizing his own divinity and invoking it to his aid. Later, this sublime and ancient truth was transformed into belief in a personal God, apart from man and from nature, and into the doctrine of vicarious atonement. But this process of change was gradual.

Early Forms of Christianity

The center of civilization at the Christian era was the Mediterranean basin, the scene of a wonderful medley of competing beliefs and cults, under the general government of the Roman Empire. There were several centers where the ancient Mysteries were preserved, taught, and practised: Alexandria, Antioch, and other places in Asia Minor; and these had communications with India and Persia. We find early Christianity maintaining the doctrines of these schools, and it has been customary to regard these forms of Christianity as heresies due to contamination from Pagan sources; which is exactly the reverse of the actual case. It is these which were the genuine

Christianity, and later Christianity was a very much expurgated derivative. So much has our attention been focussed upon the particular phase of our religion which eventually survived, that we have ignored the many other forms which for centuries rivaled it, only to succumb to the advancing materialism of the times.

Marcion, who founded the churches of the Marcionites in the second century A.D., sought to purify Christianity from the corruptions into which it had fallen. He denied the stories about Christ found in the Gospels, saying that such statements were 'carnalizations' of metaphysical allegories and a degradation of the true spiritual idea. He accused the Church Fathers of framing their doctrine according to the capacity of their hearers — "blind things for the blind according to their blindness; for the dull according to their dulness."

Manicheism was a formidable rival to the Church. Roman emperors sought to repress it, Popes anathematized it; yet for nearly a thousand years it maintained its influence, which was felt even as late as the thirteenth century by the Albigenses in southern France, who held several of its doctrines. Its founder, Mani, was of Iranian descent, born in Babylonia; and in 242 A.D. he proclaimed himself the herald of a new religion, sent forth apostles and founded congregations all over Asia Minor.

Clement of Alexandria, born about the

middle of the second century, wished to en-
rich Christianity "with the deep spirituality
of Platonism," and "advocated a Christianity
resting on free inquiry," not on faith alone.
Origen, who succeeded him, exhorted his
pupil to devote himself to Greek philosophy
as a preparatory study for Christian philosophy.

Celsus wrote his work, the *True Word*,
somewhere between 177 and 200; and what
we know of it and its author is contained in
Origen's work written in oposition to it. Celsus
maintains that Christianity is of oriental
origin; that its ethical teachings are not new;
and that many of its ceremonies are the same
as those of heathen religions. He asks why
the one God whom Christians and Pagans
alike recognize cannot be worshipped under
various names, such as Zeus, Serapis, etc. Why
should Jehovah be the only name by which
Deity can be recognized? Why did Jesus come
so late to save mankind?

Origen had been a Neo-Platonist, both he
and Plotinus having been educated in the
school of Ammonius Saccas. He was born in
185, and marks a further stage in the development of Christianity from its broad and
lofty origins towards its narrow and dogmatic
ecclesiastical form. Yet he held many doctrines since condemned as heretical: as, that
all souls are in substantial unity with God,
and not the soul of Jesus alone; that the visible universe is a manifestation of a higher

spiritual causal world. Like Paul he knew of the doctrine of hierarchies of divine beings intermediate between God and Man ('thrones, dominions, principalities, powers, etc.). The universe had a beginning, so also it must have an end; but it will be succeeded by other universes, its children — a very Theosophical doctrine.

The Gnostics, of the first three centuries, taught the *Gnosis* or Divine Knowledge, and include such names as Valentinus, Basilides, Marcion, Simon Magus. Their teachings represent a stage of Christianity when it still had teachings about the nature of the universe and of man; but when the religion became vulgarized, these teachings were condemned as heretical. Their principal teachings may be summarized as follows:

1. The opposition between spirit and matter.

2. The allegorical interpretation of Old Testament stories.

3. That the supreme God was not the God who created the world; the world was created by an inferior Aeon, called the Demiurge.

4. Jesus was not the son of Joseph and Mary, but had descended from on high; was in fact the highest of the Aeons, proceeding immediately from the Divine; he was the Redeemer not

only of man but of the world, and came to restore the original ancient Gnosis.

5. Belief in Karma and Reincarnation.

But, as this study is introductory, we cannot take more space over quotations; and must confine ourselves to a few samples which will, we hope, invite the student to follow up the subject by his own further studies. That so little is generally known about these matters is due simply to the fact that the condemnation of the churches has prevented people from studying them. But once we become aware that such information is available, we can readily assure ourselves that there is amply sufficient to establish the case. The present object is to indicate that Christianity has come down to us in a very much altered and debased form from much nobler origins.

DEVELOPMENT OF CHISTIANITY

The history of the early Christians as gathered from contemporary chroniclers of the Roman world is more familiar to the general reader. We find at first a sort of communal sect, practising high ideals of conduct; and as this grows larger, it acquires organization and becomes stratified into orders and we have the beginnings of an ecclesiastical hierarchy. The imperial authorities were tolerant or indifferent as regards religious belief, but extremely jealous of any organization which might threaten competition with the imperial sway. Trajan, though a man of broad sympathies, would not even permit the incorporation of a civic fire-brigade, for this reason.

It was thus that the Christians came in conflict with the powers that be; and the story is familiar to readers of Gibbon. It was the refusal of the Christians to enter into the ordinary life of the community, to sacrifice, to perform the usual ceremonies, to serve as soldiers, which set them apart as a dangerous sect and caused their persecution. As we know, they only grew stronger through persecution, until at last the wordly potentates were driven to make terms with the ecclesiastical ones — Clovis in the west, Roman emperors farther east. Two great factions, the Athanasians and the Arians, occupy the arena for centuries, different emperors espousing the one or the other cause; until at last the Athanasian doctrine becomes predominant in the west, the Arian in the east. Christianity is adopted by the northern conquerors of Rome, and becomes, with modifications, the religion of northern Europe.

We need not follow the story through succeeding centuries; the long and bitter struggles of the Reformation, when both parties took their faith very seriously and the temporal power was not distinguished from the spiritual, are familiar enough. We see one side resting their case on authority, supposed to have been derived by lineal descent from the apostles; the other side resting their case

on the Bible. The ghost of the Roman des-
potic imperium still survives, disputing the
field with freedom of thought; but the controversy has lost strength, as humanity is seeking its inspiration at the eternal fount — the
divine spark within the human breast.

Valentinus was the most famous Christian
teacher of the second century, and was the
instructor of the Church Fathers Origen and
Clement. It suits Christian apologists to regard him as having sought to weld together
into one, Grecian, Neo-Grecian, Jewish, and
Christian elements, and to have displayed
marvelous ingenuity and originality in so
doing. But a comparison of his doctrines with
those of other systems shows at once that
they were those of the Ancient Wisdom,
which he must have derived from the esoteric
schools then existent in Egypt and other parts
of the Mediterranean world. His school, the
Valentinians, was very influential and widespread for a long time, having main branches
in Italy and in Asia Minor, and giving rise to
several minor branches. His influence on sub-
sequent thought was very great. He averred
that the Apostles had not given out publicly all that they knew, but that they had
esoteric teachings. He teaches that the Primal
Cause, which he names *Bythos* (the Depth),
manifested itself as the *Pleroma* (Fulness),
which is the sum-total of the manifested
universe. He teaches the doctrine of divine
hierarchies, according to which the supreme

Deity emanates from himself successive orders of divine beings, to which are sometimes given such names as Archangels, Angels, Principalities, Powers, etc.; until we come to man himself, who is thus in direct descent from the Supreme Deity, and who therefore contains within himself all divine powers, which are mostly latent, but can be called forth into activity. The world in which we live was not created by the Supreme Deity, but by some of the inferior Emanations, and this explains its imperfections, which have so often been found hard to reconcile with our faith in Divine Wisdom. He gives the true teaching as to the meaning of Christ as the Divine incarnation in every man, and salvation as the reawakening of man to a knowledge of his own essential divinty.

This gives some idea of what Christianity really is and what it was at one time known to be. But when Christianity became mainly a political factor, and it was found necessary to adapt it to the needs of so many different peoples, Roman, Greek, Asiatic, Teutonic, the necessity for uniformity and for an established church with fixed doctrines caused these finer teachings to be eliminated.

III

THE BIBLE — FUNDAMENTAL
TEACHINGS: I

WHAT is the truth between the extreme views that the Bible is the literal word of God, and that it is a mass of foolish folklore? The Bible is an esoteric scripture, full of profound meaning when interpreted aright, a mere collection of stories if taken in the dead-letter sense. H. P. Blavatsky, the founder of the Theosophical Society, pays the Bible the greatest respect, but only on the condition that it be understood in the former sense. It is one of many scriptures belonging to various times and nations. It should be studied in due relation to its fellow scriptures.

We have the Old and New Testaments. The Old Testament is a collection of ancient Jewish scriptures, and we read that, after the Jews had returned from their Babylonian captivity, the scribe Ezra collected again as much as he could of the old books and re-established the Jewish canon. From this source, after other changes and eliminations, the Christian Old Testament was ultimately compiled. The Jews have their own interpretations in their Kabalistic books, such as the *Zohar* and the

Sepher Jetzirah, and a great wealth of commentaries; but the Christians know only the dead-letter sense. This has shed a bad influence on the tone of Christianity, for some of these books, literally interpreted, contain much of war, cruelty, treachery, and grossness.

The Pentateuch or first five books of the Old Testament occupies a place of special importance; though long believed to be the work of Moses, yet intelligent critism has shown that he cannot have been the author, and it is thought that they are largely the work of Ezra. Ostensibly these books contain the accounts of creation and the flood, the ancestry of the Hebrew nation, the wanderings and final settlement, and the law of Moses. The attempt to find consistency and to reconcile the narratives with other historical data is a puzzle to Biblical critics. No wonder, for it is a collection of allegorical legends put together for the main purpose of conveying the hidden meaning. But, read esoterically in the light of the *Zohar,* etc., it reveals a mine of priceless occult truths.

The Old Testament also contains the prophetic books, and *Ezekiel* and *Daniel* contain much easily recognized occult symbology, though much tortured by those who try to find in them prophecies about the second advent and the end of the world. Then there is the poetical and imaginative literature, such as *Psalms, Ecclesiastes,* and the *Song of Solomon;* and *Job,* a very ancient allegory of the trials of a candidate for initiation; it is found elsewhere and its origin is undiscoverable.

THE NEW TESTAMENT

The present canon was arrived at as the final result of a series of decisions, and is a selection out of a larger number of books, some of which are still published under the name of the Apocryphal New Testament. There were other Gospels besides the familiar four, and critics can trace back the present Gospels to older ones from which they are evidently derived. We give some quotations from *The Esoteric Character of the Gospels,* written by H. P. Blavatsky in her magazine *Lucifer* for November, 1887. [See also *Blavatsky, Collective Writings, VIII*]

. . . the Bible is *not* the "Word of God," but contains at best the words of fallible men and *imperfect* teachers. Yet read *esoterically*, it does contain, if not the *whole* truth, still, *"nothing but the truth,"* under whatever allegorical garb.

No more than any other scripture of the great world-religions can the Bible be excluded from that class of allegorical and symbolical writings which have been, from the pre-historic ages, the receptacle of the secret teachings of the Mysteries of Initiation, under a more or less veiled form. The primitive writers of the *Logia* (now the Gospels) knew certainly *the* truth, and the *whole* truth; but their successors had, as certainly, only dogma and form, which lead to hierarchical power at heart, rather than the spirit of the so-called Christ's teachings. Hence the gradual perversion.

. . . the Christian canon, especially the *Gospels*, *Acts* and *Epistles*, are made up of fragments of gnostic wisdom, the ground-work of which is pre-Christian and built on the MYSTERIES of Initiation.

. . . the more one studies ancient religious texts, the more one finds that the ground-work of the New Testament is the same as the ground-work of the Vedas, of the Egyptian theogony, and the Mazdean allegories.

Not to make too many quotations, we may say briefly that the Gospels are symbolic narratives, sacred writings, written down by unknown scribes from their recollections or notes, and afterwards compiled into a canonical collection and taken in their literal instead of their symbolic sense. But more of this will come out when we treat of the teachings under their separate headings.

As to Paul's *Epistles,* it is evident that he did not teach the representative Christian doctrines of today. The Christ, for him, is an indwelling spirit in all men; he speaks like an initiated Teacher, exhorting men to put off the old life of the flesh and to enter into the new life, wherein the Christ becomes alive and conscious in them. He is concerned with attainment and salvation in this life, not in some future life. He is evidently an adept Teacher, unable to give out all he knows, especially in open letters, and doing his best to suit his message to the capacities of the various communities he is addressing.

THE CREATION

The creation of the universe and of man occupy a foremost place in all cosmogonies and may be said to form the first chapter in the teachings of the ancient Wisdom-Religion. The word 'evolution' would be preferable to 'creation,' because the latter word is associated with the idea of a personal God creating the universe out of nothing. The subject of the evolution of worlds is treated of elsewhere, and we are concerned here only with showing it as found in the Christian Scriptures.

In the early chapters of *Genesis* (which means 'becoming' or 'begetting,' we find a rather confused and abbreviated version of what is to be found in fuller and more accurate form in older scriptures. It derives immediately from Chaldean scriptures of earlier date, some of which have been discovered by archaeologists; but it can be traced farther back to the sacred writings of ancient Persia and India. Similar accounts are to be found in China, in the mythology of ancient Scandinavia, and even among the records of ancient America. This is to mention only a few, for it is not too much to say that the same accounts of the beginnings of worlds and of the evolution of man are to be found all over the globe.

The word 'God' is in the Hebrew *elohim,* which is a plural word meaning 'gods' or 'spirits,' and refers to the creative powers. First there existed naught but Chaos, void, emptiness, often spoken of as the Waters of the Great Deep. Over this the creative spirits brood, and the first creation is Light. From these beginnings are produced the worlds and all living creatures therein. As to the creation of of man —

And the Lord God formed man of the dust of the ground, and breathed into his nostrils the breath of life; and man became a living soul. —*Genesis*, ii, 7

And God said, Let us make man in our image, after our likeness: and let them have dominion over the fish of the sea, and over the fowl of the air, and over the cattle, and over all the earth and over every creeping thing that creepeth upon the earth. So God created man in his own image, in the image of God created he him; male and female created he them. —*Genesis*, i, 26-7

As usual there are two accounts of the creation of man: he is first created a living soul (or, as more accurately translated, an animal soul) ; and then he is made divine. These two accounts have become transposed in the Authorized Version. Man has really a triple creation: first, out of the dust of the earth; then this is animated with the breath of life; last, this animal being is endowed with divine faculty — made in the image of the Gods (*elohim*). The plural word *elohim* has for some reason been translated God or Lord God; it means creative spirits, divine beings.

This teaching of the twofold creation of man is very important, as it shows how man came by his dual nature, and in what way he differs from the animal creation.

As is stated elsewhere, the early races of mankind were 'mindless,' not endowed with the self-conscious mind; and at a certain stage in evolution, the innate divinity in man was called to life by the Mânasaputras or Sons of Mind, who incarnated in the nascent human race, thus making man a self-conscious responsible being.

The story is continued in the legend of the Garden of Eden. This Garden represents the sinless innocent state of man before he became self-conscious; he was without sin, but also without the power of progress; he knew neither good nor evil. Then comes to man what has been called the Temptation. A serpent, who is discribed as very wise, appears to man and persuades him to exercise free will and rebel against God. To obtain this free will he must eat the fruit of the Tree of Knowledge of Good and Evil. He does so, and forthwith loses his state of innocent bliss, and becomes self-conscious and distinguishes between good and evil. He is cast out of the Garden and begins a life of struggle in the outer world.

This teaching has been perverted by theology into a curse and a fall; and Adam is represented to have sinned, and thereby to have communicated to all his descendants

his sin, so that all men are born in sin and
need a special divine sacrifice to save them.
But in the original teaching, the so-called
fall and temptation is a necessary stage in
the evolution of man. The Serpent (who
has been turned by theology into the Devil)
is merely God over again in another form;
for this Lord God is not the supreme deity
but those creative Spirits (*elohim*) who had
made the first unenlightened man. And the
Serpent is not the Devil but those Sons of
Mind who, as aforesaid, enlightened mankind, showing man how to partake of the
fruit of knowledge and to 'become as Gods.'
This mystery is found in the Greek mythology in the story of Prometheus, who, re-
belling against Zeus, brings fire from heaven
to enlighten man. Both the Serpent of Eden
and Prometheus are the same as Lucifer, the
Light-Bringer, who has likewise been turned
by theology into a devil.

Satan, or the Red *Fiery* Dragon, the "Lord of
Phosphorus" . . . and *Lucifer*, or "Light-Bearer," is
in us: it is our *Mind* — our tempter and Redeemer,
our intelligent Liberator and Saviour from pure ani-
malism. Without this principle — the emanation of
the very essence of the pure divine principle *Mahat*
(Intelligence) which, radiates direct from the *Divine
Mind* — we would be surely no better than animals.
The first man Adam was made only a *living soul*
(nephesh), the last Adam was made a *quickening
Spirit*: — says Paul, his words referring to the build-
ing or *Creation* of man.

— *The Secret Doctrine*, II, 513

It is the misinterpretation of this beautiful truth that has given color to the slander against human nature, whereby man is persuaded that he is naturally corrupt, is set at enmity with his own nature and made to mistrust his own intelligence and freedom of thought; it is thereby that man is cursed for performing a simple natural act, which is sinful only when perverted and associated in the mind with guilt and impurity.

This subject of the creation of man and his so-called fall connects naturally with the subject of Redemption and Salvation, another grand old teaching which has become lost during dark ages, and which has been similarly perverted into something quite different.

THE FLOOD

This is another sacred allegory common to all peoples. The story of a universal deluge, as is well known, is found everywhere, and has been supposed to be a tradition of floods following the last glaciation of parts of the northern hemisphere. And while it is perfectly true that there was an actual physical deluge — one of many, as geologists will admit — there is much more in the legend than its merely physical aspect. Daniel Brinton, in his *Myths of the New World*, has brought together a number of the flood stories of various races of ancient Americans,

north, central and south; and what is re-
markable about them is the very close simi-
larity in such details as the ark, its resting
on a mountain, the sending forth of birds.

In the Sumerian Epic of Creation, which
dates one thousand years earlier than *Genesis,* the Flood is placed before the Fall.
Flood stories, with Arks, etc., are found in
ancient India, the Norse Edda, the Finnish
Kalevala, the Mexican *Popol Vuh,* among
primitive African tribes and Polynesians. The
Greek story of Deucalion and Pyrrha, who
escaped from the Flood, and repeopled the
earth by casting stones behind them, is familiar to classical readers. The Flood story is
always connected with a purification of earth
by destruction of the wicked, and there is always an Ark or sacred vessel which preserves
a few remnants for the founding of a new
race.

Is all this physical and historical, or is it
allegorical? It is both; for the universal cor-
respondences ordain that physical events shall
be molded on spiritual events. There actually
have been periodic alterations of the earth's
surface, accompanied by the sinking of lands
and the upheaval of new lands, as indeed the
geological records show. But these events
have been but the physical accompaniments
of great moral changes; they have been
coeval with the ending of great races and the
beginning of new races of mankind; and
here we are using the word 'race' to mean

one of the great Root-Races, each of which lasts more than a million years. While the Flood has this general meaning, the innumerable accounts referred to have usually a special reference to the last great Deluge, that which accompanied the submergence of the continent of Atlantis, or to the last remaining portions thereof. This was the habitat of the Fourth Root-Race, followed by the present Fifth. The Atlantean Race having reached the end of its cycle, many of them had descended into gross materiality and were become black magicians; they were of gigantic stature, which is referred to in the Bible narrative and has given rise to the universal tradition as to wicked giants. It was necessary that this corrupt society should be destroyed, and that the good should be preserved to form the seed of the new race to come. Hence the stories of floods, arks, and the other features. The Greek mythology abounds in stories of the semi-divine founders of cities and centers of civilization, and represents these founders as having migrated into Greece from the far west "beyond the pillars of Hercules"; and there is frequent mention of the sinking of lands beneath the ocean, and the rise of other lands, on which the immigrants settled.

The fact that these deluge stories, so similar to the one in our Bible, are so universally found, is conveniently kept out of sight by most Christians, and is a stumbling-block to others, who wish to regard the Christian revelation as unique and paramount; but the problem is cleared up when we remember how the Old Testament is a compliation of ancient sacred books, which had been preserved by the Hebrews from the still older sources whence they had derived them.

REDEMPTION AND SALVATION

The drama of evolution, whether of worlds or of man, includes a descent from Spirit into Matter, and a reascent from Matter into Spirit. Man was at first spiritual, but mindless and undeveloped, living in a 'Golden Age' typified by the Garden of Eden. Then he acquires the power of self-consciousness, which is aroused within him by Beings who possessed it themselves. The Fall of man is a fall in one sense, but in another sense it is the fulfillment of a vital step in his evolution. He loses for a time his contact with Spirit, in order that he may enter on a career of incarnation in this world and pass through all its experiences. His new power of free will he misuses and brings upon himself trouble; but eventually the Divinity within him is destined to win through, so that man will rise again a much more glorious and complete being than before, because of all the added knowledge which he has garnered by his experiences. This is what is meant by Redemption and Salvation. It applies to the human race as a whole, and to particular races of mankind, and to individual men. In the case of individual men we must of course take into account reincarnation.

And so the world's great Teachers have at many times come into our world to preach anew the glad tidings, or rather to remind man of his forgotten birthright. For man is like some prince in an old story, who has been brought up among peasants, so that he is unaware of his royalty; though even in dark ages there have always been a few mystics and intuitive minds who have perceived the truth. The Wise One who initiated Christianity (whoever he was) was one of these Teachers; and even in the mutilated fragments of his teachings which remain to us we can see that he was proclaiming that old truth. Yet see what ages of spiritual darkness have made of it! Whereas the Teacher proclaimed the divinity of man, and showed to his hearers the age-old path to salvation, we are told today that we are essentially corrupt and that it is impious to rely on our own resources — we, created in God's own image! Truly Theosophy has come to raise the buried Christ from the tomb wherein his disciples have cast him. For Theosophy is just such another revival of the Wisdom-Religion, two thousand years later; and what Jesus said of the Pharisees of his day might be applied to much that goes today under the name of religion.

The Atonement, or making 'at one,' is theologically regarded as a reconciliation between God and man, due to the propitiation of his Son; but in the light of what has been said the word acquires a truer sense. It means the uniting of the human ego with the Spiritual Ego — the innate Christ, whereby man recognizes that this Spiritual Ego, and not his personal ego, is his true Self.

SACRAMENTS: THE EUCHARIST

And he took bread, and gave thanks, and brake it, and gave unto them, saying, This is my body, which is given for you: this do in remembrance of me. Likewise also the cup after supper, saying, This cup is the new testament in my blood, which is shed for you. —*Luke*, xxii, 19-20

Then Jesus said unto them, Verily, verily I say unto you, Except ye eat the flesh of the Son of man, and drink his blood, ye have no life in you. Whoso eateth my flesh, and drinketh my blood, hath eternal life; and I will raise him up at the last day. For my flesh is meat indeed, and my blood is drink indeed. He that eateth my flesh, and drinketh my blood, dwelleth in me, and I in him.
—*John*, vi, 53-6

The sacrament of the Lord's Supper means much to those who partake of it devoutly, but it might mean much more. Its sacredness and power are due to its august origin from one of the sublimest rites of the Sacred Mysteries of old. Its frailty as a potent influence for good in the world, its rôle as a bone of bitter contention, are due to the attenuated and misunderstood form in which it has come down to us. If we study the ancient Mysteries, we find that bread and wine play a foremost part in the ritual of initiation, as also in the 'Lesser Mysteries' which were displayed before the public. In the Greater Mysteries candidates were initiated into what Jesus calls the Kingdom of God or the Kingdom of Heaven, into which he seems anxious that his disciples should be initiated. Wine is often spoken of alternatively with blood, and both signify spiritual life: the words are thus used in the New Testament. Over against these we find bread or grain, or alternatively flesh; and these words also are used in the New Testament. This latter signifies terrestrial mortal life; so that the two together mean the higher and lower nature of man.

The reference is to symbols which were used in the ancient Mysteries, in which there was a twofold initiation, symbolized respectively by bread and wine, or by flesh and blood. The candidate had to be pure in body and the lower principles of his nature, before receiving the baptism of blood or the wine of the spirit. These facts relative to the Greek and other Mysteries can be verified by reference to any encyclopaedia or book on the subject. In the Bible we find frequent reference thereto. Besides the two quotations at the head of this section, we may cite the interview with Nicodemus in *John,* iii:

Except a man be born again, he cannot see the kingdom of God. . . . Except a man be born of water and of the Spirit, he cannot enter into the kingdom of God. That which is born of the flesh is flesh: and that which is born of the Spirit is spirit.

Here we see the double birth; the first of flesh, the second of Spirit. This doctrine of the second birth is of course the principal theme of Paul, and it is surprising that so little is made of it; at most it is regarded as referring to a state of mind or heart varying from mere self-satisfaction to a real holiness of character. But the real meaning is quite lost owing to belief in original sin and vicarious atonement and an ignorance of reincarnation.

These ancient teachings are immortal, which is why they survive through the ages, if only in form, until the time comes for them to be restored. The Eucharist is still celebrated as a means of receiving divine grace and as a commemoration, and some attach great importance to the faith in a miraculous transubstantiation of the bread and wine into the actual flesh and blood of Jesus.

SACRAMENTS: BAPTISM

This is another rite derived from the ancient Mysteries. It was the outer and visible form of a purificatory process undergone by the candidate for initiation. Initiatory ablutions are common to all cults. In Christianity it means admission to the Church, and is regarded as cleansing from sin, affiliating with God, and the gift of the Spirit. That those who have not been baptized will suffer damnation is a formal article of faith with some. The idea is repugnant to the feelings of the present day; but if we can be saved without baptism, why be baptized?

Sacraments are defined in the Catechism as the outward and visible sign of an inward and spiritual grace; they repeat physically what has already occurred spiritually; otherwise the ceremony is but an empty form. There are two baptisms: that of water and that of fire; corresponding with the two forms of the Eucharist already mentioned. It would seem that the candidate for baptism should be of an age suitable to the full understanding of the meaning of the ceremony. In these days, when our knowledge of nature is so restricted to externals, we have lost sight of that intimate knowledge of nature, of man, and of man's relation to nature, which was possessed in more ancient times. The rites and customs of which we read in Greek and Roman history, or as practised in ancient and oriental races, seem to us superstition, because we do not grasp their real meaning; and it is quite likely that the Greeks and Romans themselves in later times had lost it also and continued the ceremonies merely from custom. But a further study shows that they originated in the teachings of the Ancient Wisdom. It is curious that we still go on practising them; but there is an undying life in these ancient institutions, which preserves them through the ages, like a seed under the snow, until the time comes round for them to be revivified.

IV

THE BIBLE — FUNDAMENTAL TEACHINGS: II

REINCARNATION

A S the doctrine of Reincarnation and its twin doctrine of Karma form so important a part of the Ancient Wisdom from which all religions have descended, it is important to know why we find so little of it in Christianity. The simple reason is that it has been expurgated. A learned scholar, the late Professor F. S. Darrow, writes:

The critical history of the doctrines of Pre-exist-ence and Reincarnation has never been written, but the materials at hand for such a history are most extensive. I have in my library, without the slightest exaggeration, literally *hundreds* of volumes having to do with this subject. Many of the volumes deal entirely with that subject and nothing else. . . . The Theo-sophical teachings in regard to the pre-existence and rebirth of the human soul have been plainly and con-tinuously enunciated in the Christian world from the very beginning of Christianity until the present day, but the recognition of these truths among professed Christians naturally has varied greatly from time to time in accordance with the degree of publicity per-mitted by the pendulum swing of the cycles.

The same author divides the subject chronologically into three heads: The period of early Christianity until the Synod of Constantinople in 553, which officially declared the teachings of the Church Father Origen in regard to the nature and destiny of the soul to be 'heretical'; from 553 to 1438, when Georgious Gemistus visited Florence and revived the philosophy of Plato; thence down to modern times.

So the only reason why this knowledge of pre-existence and reincarnation is not heard of is that it has never been studied; the literature is there in abundance, but having been banned as heretical it has been neglected. The reason why these teachings have been banned is easy to see. Their admission would open the door to so very much that is incompatible with ecclesiastical Christianity. And so we have to get along with the absurdity that souls are created at a point in time, and yet live for ever; that they survive the body but did not pre-exist it; and the utter insignificance of a life of seventy years amid the ocean of eternity. These topics however are discussed in the manual on Reincarnation (No. 2 of this series).

The Christian scheme, as generally understood today, affords no explanation for the inequalities and incompleteness of human life, other than attributing them to the inscrutable will of a personal deity. This denies to man his speculative instinct, his thirst of knowledge; thus leaving him to seek satisfaction therefor outside the pale of religion, and to have more than one religion at the same time, and a second God called 'Nature.' His innate sense of justice rebels against what he has been constrained to believe; his study of nature has given him the idea of law and order; but his religious teaching, instead of confirming, thwarts these — good reason for surmising that his religion has come down to him in adulterated form. Instead of discarding the whole thing, let him reinstate it, rejecting what is false and holding to what is true.

THE DOCTRINE OF THE TRINITY

The Father, the Son, and the Holy Ghost —three Persons and yet only one God. Such is the Christian Trinity; and bitter controversies have raged as to the exact nature of this triune God and the relations of the three Persons to each other. The entire Christian world, in Roman times, was divided by irreconcilable schism turning on the question whether the Son was of the same substance with the Father, or of like substance with the Father. Is the Son co-eternal with the Father, or was he produced from the Father? It is customary to accuse the disputants with raising a turmoil over trifles, but this is unfair, for great issues may turn on a very small point of symbolism, and this difference about the creed was the sign by which were distinguished from one another two bodies of Christians whose general attitude was antagonistic.

Why was the Deity thus represented as a Three-in-One? The doctrine is not to be found formally stated in the New Testament; it was devised by Church Councils who formulated the creed, and the terms used in the formula are not Biblical. But once formulated, it could be justified by reference to the New Testament.

The fact is that such a triune deity is found at the head of all theogonies and cosmogonies; and philosophical systems usually begin with something equivalent. In the very beginning of the Bible it is represented as the Spirit of God, brooding over the waters of Space or Chaos, and bringing forth the universe. This is the great creative trinity which stands at the head of cosmogonies: a Universal Spirit, Father of all; then comes the Chaos or the Great Depth or the Waters of Space, which is often called the great Mother. From these two proceed the Son, which is the universe. This philosophical trinity, which is indeed a necessity of thought, was naturally enough adopted by the Church; its adoption put them into harmony with all the other religions and philosophies, with Greek thought especially, and with various Eastern systems current in Asia Minor. The persons of this Trinity could then be readily found in the New Testament, for Jesus often speaks of

the Father and the Son, and of the Holy
Spirit which he will send.

But this Trinity is defective, for there is
a Father and a Son, but no Mother. In one
church this last is supplied by the Virgin,
though she is not a member of the Trinity.
The Virgin is taken from the Magna Mater,
or Great Mother, so much reverenced in
many of the Asiatic religions prevalent in
parts of the Roman empire; but indeed there
is always a Great Mother, regarded as the
consort of the Father, whether it is Hera,
consort of Zeus; Juno, consort of Jupiter;
Isis, consort of Osiris and Mother of Horus;
or what not.

In ordinary Christian belief the Father
and the Son have been personalized, and the
Holy Ghost or Holy Spirit is a somewhat
vague conception. What is called inspiration
is in many cases a mere neurotic excitement,
with disastrous reactions; but there have always been Christian mystics who have attained to a higher realization of the meaning
of inspiration. We are aware that some
readers of this may point to the fine charac-
ters and noble lives of many devout and
earnest Christians, but we prefer to attribute
this to the innate nobility of human nature,
which has enabled these persons to imbibe
the true spirit of their religion in spite of
its defects. Under a better understanding of
Christianity there would be more of such
people.

THE CROSS

And he bearing his cross went forth to a place
called the place of a skull . . . where they crucified
him. —*John*, xiy, 17-18

The preaching of the cross is to them that perish
foolishness; but unto us who are saved it is the
power of God.—1 *Cor.*, i, 18

If any man will come after me, let him deny himself, and take up his cross, and follow me.

—*Matt.*, xiv, 24

The above are typical examples of the use
of the word 'cross' in the New Testament;
it means the stake used in crucifixion, or the
Christian doctrine, or a burden or sacrifice.
This sacred symbol of Christianity is a per-
petual reminder of its cardinal doctrine that
Christ died for our sins, whereby we are
saved. It is also used for the daily burden
we take up in sacrificing our personal will
to our faith.

But the cross is a universal religious and
philosophical symbol, found in places as re-
mote as Palenque in Mexico, India, and
Tibet; well known in Egyptian symbolism, as
in Hindûism; an emblem used in the sacred
Mysteries of ancient Greece. Dr. Lundy, in
his *Monumental Christianity,* says that "the
Jews themselves acknowledged this sign of
salvation until they rejected Christ"; and he
speaks of a Hindû sculpture of ancient date,
a human figure upon a cross, with the nail-
marks on hands and feet — a pre-Christian
crucifix in fact.

Theosophy shows that the teachings of the Ancient Wisdom were preserved in a universal symbol-language, which conveyed the leading tenets; and the cross is one of these symbols, which is why it is so universally found. The Sun, Moon, and Cross form a trinity of symbols, denoting respectively Father, Mother, Son; Cosmic Spirit, Cosmic Matter, and the universe produced by their interaction. In the case of Man, who is a miniature copy of the universe, the cross denotes what John calls the Word made Flesh, the Son, the Christ, which is in every man and is the divine part of his nature.

In order to explain why such a symbol was chosen to represent this idea, we should have to go more deeply into matters than is appropriate here; but it may be stated that the two lines of the cross (speaking particularly of the Greek cross with four equal arms) stand for Spirit and Matter, and the fact of their crossing each other denotes the union or interaction of these two elements to form the manifested universe. The Divine Spirit in man is said to be crucified, made into a cross, caused to dwell in a residence of flesh; and this crucifixion is destined to be succeeded by resurrection.

It is also to be observed that a ceremony of crucifixion was actually performed upon the candidates for initiation into the Sacred Mysteries, which still existed in some parts of the Roman world at the Christian era.

These candidates, at a certain stage in their initiation, were fastened to a cross or cruciform couch, where they lay entranced for two days, while their liberated Soul went through the necessary experiences, and came to life again on the third day. It is possible that the story in the Gospels was founded on this. However, the Christians have taken over the cross and adopted it as their symbol; the other two, the sun and moon, are seen in the emblems of Japan and Islam.

But this meaning of the cross has become confused or blended with that of the Roman instrument of capital punishment, which was a stake, usually with a cross-bar near the top, to which the criminal was fastened. Whether there really was a teacher who, after a very short ministry, was apprehended, condemned, and thus executed, may be doubted. There is no historical record to substantiate it.

The crucifixion of the Christ is the symbolic name for a cardinal tenet of the Ancient Wisdom; but it has been materialized into the story of an actual crucifixion of Jesus by Pontius Pilatus in the reign of Tiberius. Critical people, doubting the authenticity of this story, or doubting its importance even if authentic, have gone too far in their objections and thrown over Christianity itself, and even all religion; which shows how important it is to separate the true from the false and to avoid literal and materialistic interpretation of spiritual truths couched in symbolic language.

The sign of the cross has become a sacred *emblem,* a sign which has value through the association of ideas; and in the use of the pious and of mystics has been a potent means of invoking spiritual aid, though also at times a standard of war. To the above it may be added that the cross is a better symbol when drawn within the circle or with a circle joined to the upper arm. The circle stands for Spirit, and the cross alone denotes materialism, which may be said to be characteristic of the times wherein Christianity has been prevalent; these times being characterized, as said, by the interpreting of mystic symbols in a literal sense.

THE MYSTERIES

In ancient Greece were the Mysteries of Eleusis and other schools of the Mysteries less well known; where candidates for initiation were received. Such schools existed also in Egypt, India, and several other places, and connections can be traced between the schools in these different localities, whereby confirmation is obtained of the fact that they taught a uniform doctrine. This was the Secret Doctrine or Wisdom-Religion, of which Theosophy is the modern expression. As man is essentially divine, being a lineal descendant through evolution from divine beings, it is possible for him by a particular course of training to arouse the latent spiritual powers within him. This is called the Path of Wisdom, and is in fact Salvation in the real sense of that word. The Gospels contain sufficient evidence that the Teacher whose words are quoted therein was aware of the existence of this Path and that he wished his disciples to follow it. He calls it the Kingdom of God. It is also stated that he gave his disciples secret instructions apart from the multitude.

At the time of the Christian era there still existed some of these Mystery-Schools in Egypt and parts of Asia, and their influence is evident in the doctrines of the Gnostics, Neo-Platonists, and similar cults, among which Christianity was developed. The process of selection and compilation which resulted in the canonical Gospels led to an inclusion of extracts from these teachings, and the putting of them into the mouth of the Teacher called Jesus.

Paul, who seems to have written his epistles before the Gospel narratives were drawn up, interprets the Christian doctrines in a much more esoteric way. One would judge from his manner of speaking that he himself was initiated, to some degree at least; but he was clearly under the necessity of adapting his teachings to the limited comprehension of his various hearers, and he often uses figurative language whose real sense would only be understood by a few of those whom he addressed.

THE SECOND COMING OF CHRIST

From the Gospel narratives, and from what history tells us, we gather that there was among the early Christians a widespread and often very confident belief that Christ would really come again in the flesh, and that very soon, to destroy evil and set up a kingdom of the righteous on earth. This idea was connected with the decay of the Roman empire, which figured as the evil dominion that Christ was to overthrow; and it is no wonder that these Christians excited the jealousy of Roman rulers.

The Jews too, who contributed so many Christians, and whose influence entered so largely into Christian ideas, had their own prophecies of the return of one or another of their own prophets as the 'Messiah'; and this idea evidently contributed largely to the belief as to the return of Christ. Some Biblical critics are convinced that Jesus himself, at one time at least, believed this; but we have to bear in mind that the Gospels, as they have come down to us, were largely made to order.

A most indisputable instance of this is to be found in *Matthew,* xxiv, 3, which the *Authorized Version* translates quite wrongly from the Greek, but which is translated correctly in the *Revised Version,* which was made by a body of divines and scholars in 1881. A comparison of these two renderings will show that the earlier translators have twisted the Greek original into a confirmation of their views about the second coming. The passages are as follows:

Authorized Version: And as he sat upon the mount of Olives, the disciples came unto him privately, saying, Tell us, when shall these things be? and what shall be the sign of thy coming, and of the end of the world?

Revised Version: . . . the sign of thy presence, and of the consummation of the age?

This latter is the meaning of the Greek, and the former is a forced rendering.*

We see here an allusion to the doctrine of cycles, in accordance with which great Root-Races of humanity succeed one another. The 'Consummation of the age' is when the present Root-Race† has run its course, and humanity will be divided into those who have progressed enough to form the nucleus of the next succeeding Race, and those who have

---

*While on this subject, it is worth noting that the passage *Mark*, xvi, 9-20, does not occur in most of the manuscript and is regarded as a spurious insertion. It contains the words: "He that believeth and is baptized shall be saved; but he that believeth not shall be damned."

†See manual No. VII of the series: *Man's Divine Parentage and Destiny: The Great Rounds and Races.*

lagged in the rear of progress. This latter part of the Race will come to an end (as a race), in the cataclysms which separate one Race from another; while the others will be 'saved,' as is figured in the allegory of the Flood and the Ark. Jesuse in his answer says that the end is not yet, there will be wars, there will be many false prophets. The Coming of Christ means the reawakening of the Christ spirit in mankind or in as many as are able to receive it.

There are Adventists among the Christians of today, who still expect an actual physical coming of Christ; and there are some who interpret the Books of *Daniel* and *Ezekiel* and and *Revelation* in that sense. But though these prophecies do relate to great cyclic changes, and though the Adventists have the intuition that such changes impend, they are too literal and materialistic in their interpretation.

The Golden Rule

This is often cited as characteristc of Christianity, but it is known to exist in all other religions. To the Theosophist it is more than a mere moral injunction; it is a necessary law of man's nature. For man, essentially divine, having wandered away from the knowledge of his own divinity, has to regain it. His great obstacle is self-love; therefore he can only regain his lost kingdom by over-

coming self-love. So he must somehow find
out how to act from an impersonal motive.
It is evident, therefore, that ideas of self-
advancement, of gaining occult powers for
his own satisfaction, or even the desire for
personal holiness, will never suffice, because
the indulgence of such desires is merely increasing the power of the enemy we wish to
conquer. To exchange a weak personality for
a strong one cannot be the way. But a large
part of our daily lives is composed of actions
into which self-love does not enter — disin-
terested actions, actions prompted by a genuine and uncalculating desire to serve another or others. Or perhaps, having witnessd the
pain caused to others by some selfish action
of ours, and feeling remorse therefor, we have
registered a resolve not to act thus in the
future, a resolve prompted by no thought of
self-benefit whatever, but simply by the desire
to avoid wronging other people.

The motive which operates in these cases
is that of Love — not passional love but
pure impersonal love. This is a cosmic force.
It operates in the animal world; for that
which we so disparagingly call 'instinct' is
truly a pure and simple manifestation of a
great cosmic force leading the beast to sacrifice itself for its offspring, the dog to die
unhesitatingly for his master. The Teacher
in the Gospels upholds the simple, the beasts
and birds, the lilies of the field, and the
children; as well he might, and as we often

feel disposed to do after experiences of human selfishness.

So the Teacher, in enunciating the Golden Rule, merely points out to those who aspire to fulfil the true destiny of man the law of the spiritual life, of the Kingdom of Heaven; which is harmony, not strife. This is a path which the individual may enter upon at any time, and which humanity in the aggregate must one day follow; though there will always be some who, having failed to attain the ideal, will miss their chance for one cycle and have to await another opportunity for progress. It has been said that the teachings of the Sermon on the Mount are impracticable and would result in the dissolution of society; but they set forth the ideal, and it is precisely the possession of such an ideal which prevents man from sinking under the load of his difficulties. As for ways and means of reforming society, perhaps if we began by setting our own house in order we might thereby gain vision and power towards that end.

The Golden Rule shows the way of realizing the unity of living beings; and this is specially brought out in the injunctions to forgive our neighbor. But if this is only to mean that we suppress our anger towards him, while still continuing to imagine ourself his victim, the real forgiveness has not been achieved. In the greater fullness of life to which we aspire, and to which the

Teacher points the way, we shall see that our neighbor is actually part of our own Self, and then all feelings of animosity or conflict will seem absurd. In our present darkness we have falsely separated a unity into two halves, one of which is supposed to have been injured by the other. Forgiveness consists in the dispelling of this illusion.

This Rule is the prime maxim of conduct for the disciple in any system of practical religion or philosophy which aims at self-realization, and which sets before the aspirant the Path of Wisdom and Attainment. And truly it must be so; for it is self-seeking which binds a man down to the illusions and frustrations of his mortal life; and to escape, it is necessary to give up this law or self-seeking in favor of a higher law. It may be said, perhaps, that the strict following out of such a law, in the way (for instance) of the Sermon on the Mount, is too much to ask of an ordinary man. But, while the heights may be left to the comparatively few who feel themselves ready to scale them, even the most ordinary man is every moment faced with the choice between selfish and unselfish conduct, and must choose the one course or the other. With the ideal ever before him, and with an understanding of its rationality, he will be enabled to choose the right course, thus preparing himself for what awaits him in the future. For the day must come for every man when compromise will

no longer be possible and he must choose
definitely which path he will take. Never
was the practice of unselfishness more needed than today, and it will help people to
achieve it if they are not hampered by materialistic forms of religion and science which
accentuate the lower aspect of human nature.

THE IMMANENT CHRIST

This means the Christ that dwells in every
human heart, as distinct from the man Christ
who is said to have been crucified. The doctrine of the indwelling Christ is taught in
the Gospels and in Paul's Letters, so it is to
be found in the Bible and in Christianity
by those willing to look for it. Those who
prefer the anthropomorphized ecclesiastical
doctrine of the crucifixion of a particular man
will have to consider these Biblical teachings
as figurative. Yet it would be a mistake to
judge Christianity by its crudest forms, and
it is true that many enlightened and broad-
church teachers adopt this doctrine of the
indwelling Christ, and that many devout
Christians approximate in varing degrees to
it. There are many to whom the life of Christ
as represented in the Gospels has been an
ideal and a pattern on which they have
sought to mold their own lives; and saints
and mystics have attained to high levels by
contemplation of this ideal. But this is not
enough; there still remains the notion that

man is a weak creature, born in sin, and looking for salvation beyond the grave; and that
it would be presumptuous in him to attempt
really to imitate Christ. Yet in the original
teaching the Christ means the Divine Spirit
resident in the core of our being, the Christ
which has been sacrificed and entombed and
has to be resurrected in us. Certain great
Teachers may be described in a special sense
as Christs, inasmuch as they have attained to
a self-realization to which the majority have
not yet attained. But they do not set themselves up as the *only* son of God, but merely
offer their lives as a pattern for other people
to follow. In the real doctrine we are all sons
of God in the same way as Jesus was, and
can really achieve what he achieved, as he
himself promises when he says:

> He that believeth on me, the works that I do shall
> he do also; and greater works than these shall he do;
> because I go unto my Father.
>
> —*John*, xiv, 12

This indwelling Christ is called 'The Son';
and the Divine Spirit is called 'The Father.'

> No man knoweth the Son, but the Father; neither
> knoweth any man the Father, save the Son, and he to
> whomsoever the Son will reveal him.
>
> —*Matthew*, xi, 27

On this point we may quote from 'The
Esoteric Character of the Gospels,' by H. P.
Blavatsky, as follows:

The first key that one has to use to unravel the dark secrets involved in the mystic name of Christ, is the key which unlocked the door to the ancient mysteries of the primitive Aryans, Sabeans, and Egyptians. The Gnosis supplanted by the Christian scheme was universal. It was the echo of the primordial wisdom-religion which had once been the heirloom of the whole of mankind; and, therefore, one may truly say that, in its purely metaphysical aspect, the Spirit of Christ (the divine *logos*) was present in humanity from the beginning of it. The author of the Clementine Homilies is right; the mystery of Christos — now supposed to have been taught by Jesus of Nazareth — "was identical" with that which *from the first* had been communicated *"to those who were worthy."* . . .

These and other words used—

apply to all those who, without being Initiates, strive and succeed, through personal efforts to *live the life* and to attain the naturally ensuing spiritual illumination in blending their personlity — the ("Son") with (the "Father,") their individual divine Spirit, *the God within* them.

Compare this with the Bible itself:

Know ye not, that so many of us as were baptized into Jesus Christ were baptized into his death? Therefore we are buried with him by baptism into death: that like as Christ was raised up from the dead by the glory of the Father, even so we also should walk in newness of life. For if we have been planted together in the likeness of his death, we shall be also in the likeness of his resurrection: knowing this, that our old man is crucified with him, that the body of sin might be destroyed, that henceforth we should not serve sin. For he that is dead is freed from sin. Now if we be dead with Christ, we believe that we shall also live with him. —*Romans*, vi, 3-8

The first man is of the earth, earthy: the second man is the Lord from Heaven.

—1 *Corinthians,* xv, 47

As in Adam all die, so in Christ shall all be made alive. —1 *Corinthians,* xv, 22

Adam, in Hebrew, means 'earthy'; it stands for the terrestrial nature of man; but the allegory has been literalized; the type figure has been turned into an actual individual man. But Paul here uses it in the right symbolic sense. Contrasted with this is the heavenly man — Christ — the divine part of human nature. The one is mortal, the other immortal. But does this refer to a state of perfection after death? By no means, for the teaching is that we can attain it while on earth. Earth is the place where man achieves; he is here to learn its lessons and to win victory over its forces. This state of attainment, whereby we cease to be dead with Adam, and become alive with Christ, is called the Second Birth.

In *Matthew,* iii, 11, John the Baptist says:

I indeed baptize you with water unto repentance: but he that cometh after me is mightier than I, whose shoes I am not worthy to bear: he shall baptize you with the Holy Ghost, and with fire.

Turn now to *John,* iii, where a rabbi comes privately to Jesus, asking what is meant by the saying that a man must be born again; and is told:

Except a man be born again, he cannot see the kingdom of God.

But can a man enter the womb a second time? asks Nicodemus; and is answered:

Except a man be born of water and of the Spirit, he cannot enter into the kingdom of God. That which is born of the flesh is flesh: and that which is born of the Spirit is spirit.

It is needless to burden this book with multiplied quotations, but the frequent references to the Kingdom of God (or Heaven) are well enough known. It is evident that this expression refers to a state attainable by man while on earth, and that the sayings in the Gospels, whatever their original source, are those of a teacher of the Ancient Wisdom. They have been construed to refer to a state of bliss after death, which is not sufficiently vivid to affect the minds of most people, and does not fit in with the general scheme of things which we infer from our knowledge of nature and life.

V

CHRISTIANITY AND MORALITY

PEOPLE may wonder if the abandonment of Christianity (as ordinarily understood) will mean a loss of the basis of moral conduct and a consequent general, if gradual, lapse into profligacy of various kinds. This is a quesion which demands serious consideration and cannot be dismissed with a few bald assertions. Rationalists, Secularists, and others of that genus, say that the fount of good conduct is in the human intelligence and instincts, that religion is rather a hindrance than a help, and that this fount will suffice for needs. But to this it can be answered that perhaps these rationalists are living on the capital of good habits accumulated by centuries of religious influence, that this capital would soon become exhausted, and that the the human intellect and instinct, as conceived by rationalism, would not suffice to renew the stock.

Here indeed is the weakness of the rationalist and humanist position. Their philosophy lacks foundations; and if pressed on this point, they are too ready to take refuge in agnosticism — the view that these fundamental questions lie byond the scope of inquiry, that they cannot be known, that it is needless to try to fathom them. We seem to detect here the scientific fallacy of confusing cause with effect: is morality a cause or an effect? Is it any use saying that morality is the effect of morality? Or if, to avoid such tautology, we change the wording and say that morality is the effect of human intelligence and instinct, we have merely dodged the difficulty.

We need to know something about those mysterious powers in the human breast. By what are they inspired? Shall we define them as an enlightened self-interest? In that case we commit ourselves to the proposition that morality is sustained by self-interest, and that self-interest is the foundation of human conduct. The forces which rule in matter must themselves be immaterial, outside of matter; otherwise we are reasoning in a circle and have an engine generating its own steam, or a motor and a dynamo running each other. And so with the present problem. Human social conduct cannot be represented as a mechanism perpetually running by its own momentum; it could never rise, and would be much more likely to fall. It is clear that this 'Unknowable' which the rationalists admit but scorn to inquire into, is the very mainspring.

Here is where religion comes in. The rationalists have thrown away the grain with the chaff. It is the *spirit* of religion, Religion itself, which keeps alive the eternal vitality of the human race, compelling obedience to the essential laws of moral health, and preventing an utter collapse into destruction by unrelieved selfishness.

And this true Religion has its shrine in the human heart. But a pious, devotional, emotional attitude will not suffice to keep the fire alive in an age where the intellect is so acute. This intellect has been enlisted on the side of self-interest, with the results which we so much dread. Unless the scope of the intellect can be expanded so as to inquire into and learn about those parts of human nature which lie below the surface, we shall become morally bankrupt. To live healthfully in a physical sense, we must know the laws of hygiene and sanitation; we cannot go by blind faith and guesswork. And this deeper knowledge is what Religion can and should give us.

That Christianity has failed so much as it has in this respect is due to the great admixture of dross with the pure metal. We have sought in this book to bring out the essential truths in Christianity, and to explain them in a way which will be more vital and effectual in human life. We have not taken away from man anything needed for his support. Whatever can be said in favor of the influence of Christianity can be said with greater force with regard to the Theosophical interpretation of Christianity. We have expressly said that we have no wish to interfere with the faith of those who find in their religion what they need and who seek nothing further; and that our object is to help those for whom this is not sufficient, and who are earnestly seeking for the real basis of human welfare.

Religion which teaches man that he is essentially divine cannot be more immoral in its influence than religion which teaches him he is a miserable sinner. In the Theosophical interpretation of Christianity the moral law is the essential law of human conduct, by which alone man can achieve happiness, self-realization, and harmony of his life with that of his fellows. It is this interpretation alone which unifies life and brings into harmony intellect and heart, so that all our faculties may co-operate towards the end of perfection.

God

God is not a person standing outside the universe. Nor is he apart from man. God is everywhere: there is nothing which is not God. God is the ultimate fact, the root of all existence, the spiritual foundation of all that is. Many thinkers have arrived at this conception of God, and have realized that the theological God is an anthropomorphized ideal. God, the universe, man, are not separate from each other, but form a unity. We can approach God only by sounding the depths of our own being; for man himself is a manifestation of Divinity, and there are no limits to what he can attain through self-knowledge.

The manifold objections to the idea of a personal and extracosmic God are almost too well known to need mention. Such a God seems to manifest little interest in human affairs, and to be apart from Nature, which is a sort of secondary deity. It is little wonder that so many have abandoned the idea of God altogether, though it passes comprehension to understand how these explain the meaning of things. To abandon the idea of God does not mean that we must represent the universe as a haphazard mechanism.

The doctrine of extreme materialism means nothing; agnosticism is a confession of ignorance and helplessness. We may call ourselves Humanists, and make man the center of things; but then what is man? Every man, studying the wonders of his own conscious being, knows that there is a profound mystery beyond the limits of thought. But to suppose that that mystery is utterly insoluble is to turn the whole universe and human life into a horrible jest.

There have always been Christian mystics, who have taught that revelation comes through self-communion. This is the only way to knowledge of God; and, as we have shown, Jesus points the way to the attainment of such knowledge. There are faculties in man which transcend the intellect (as we know it now) — not set it aside or abrogate it, but supplement it. Man little knows the sublimity of his own nature, though many of us have at rare moments obtained glimpses. Let us aspire to the highest we can attain, and forbear to limit our vision by giving it the form of a personal deity, which is in very truth creating a graven image.

Prayer

Supplication to a personal deity for favors desired is looking for help in the wrong place. It is presuming to dictate to deity and is based on the idea that divine goodness and wisdom needs the help of our prayers. The climax of absurdity is reached when hostile armies pray for victory over each other. This brings out the truth that a personal God is usually partial, local, tribal. There is some sense in such invocations if we believe that each nation has its own special deity, as some peoples believe; but it becomes nonsense when such contradictory prayers are addressed to one and the same God.

Prayer means self-communion accompanied by high aspiration, and should be in the spirit of 'Not my will, but thine be done.' Prayer for specific objects is not right, because we do not know what is best for us. Prayer is communing with the Father in Heaven through the Son; reaching towards our own highest and best. Personal wishes must be cast aside, and the unity of life realized as much as possible.

The Problem of Evil

People often vex themselves with the question how a good God can permit evil. Evil is imperfection, and this world is but an imperfect manifestation of Deity the All-Good. Contrast and opposition are found everywhere; they are necessary conditions of growth and experience. Evil has been defined as the shadow of God. Attempts to define good and evil philosophically have not much bearing upon duty and conduct, and usually serve merely to bewilder people. In actual life good and evil are as distinct as a good egg and a bad egg. Every man is naturally endowed with the ability to distinguish them.

The words good and evil are very vague, and confusion arises from their being used in varying senses. They may be taken to mean pleasant and unpleasant; but this obviously refers to our tastes, which are unreliable as criterions. What is unpleasant may be good for us; what is pleasant, evil. They may be taken to mean right and wrong, and here again the reference may be to moral law, or social law, or civic law, etc.

As far as our own experiences are concerned, the true philosopher can arrive at a state where he recognizee that no evil can befall him, because he accepts every event as a part of his equitable lot — the Stoic philosophy. So we see that in this case the terms good and evil imply a contrast which we have made in our own minds, by classifying experiences as pleasant and unpleasant, and speaking of good and evil fortune.

As long as a man makes personal pleasure an object, he is bound to bring pain upon himself, by the same law which renders the glutton or the drunkard sick. Such pursuit of self-gratification upsets the moral balance, and Nature restores it by the complementary opposite experience. But what about our conduct to other people? This ought surely to concern most a person of heart and conscience; and it might be better if people spoke more about this aspect of the question than about their own luck and ill-luck and merit and demerit, which are utterly trivial to anybody but themselves.

Can it be denied that we have the power to work evil upon our fellows? And if there is anyone whose mind has become so disordered that he can argue, "Whatever happens to a man is his Karma; therefore I cannot injure him," and use this as an excuse for misbehavior; then we can only pity such a man. To do mischief in the world and leave it to the universal laws of harmony to clean up the mess we have made, is but a sorry way of manifesting the divinity that is in us. So far as our conduct to others is concerned, there is an unmistakable difference between good and evil, and an inescapable obligation upon every man who *is* a man to choose the right. And if he *is* a man, he will do the right despite all the religions and philosophies in the world.

As said above, in speaking of the Fall of Man, the making of Deity into a personal God has necessitated the making of a personal Satan as the adversary of God. But, as there stated, the Serpent of Eden was man's Teacher, who awoke in him the power of intelligence; and when this Serpent is called the Adversary, it means that he was opposed to the first God who created man as an unintelligent though sinless being.

Satan is also a personification of our passions, which seek to lead us to destruction; but it is by fighting them that we learn and progress, so that ultimately they become our savior. But that is only on condition that we fight and overcome them; if we yield to them we are lost. There is no Devil with horns and hoofs, haunting us during life and preparing to torment us after death. But it is only too true that our passions, allied to our intellect, can create a kind of secondary evil self, which is our enemy whom we must conquer. It is also true that the Astral Light is full of destructive powers engendered by the thoughts and passions or men; so that the Astral Light, in one of its aspects, has merited the title of Satan.

CONCLUSION

O UR subject is so large that we have not attempted to comprehend it; and had we done so, we should but have wearied the reader's attention. However, enough has been said to invite the interested student to further study of the subject. The evidences for the views taken here are abundant and will be forthcoming in future years; they have been ignored because they have not suited the plans of the custodians of sectarian religion. But, once broader views prevail, as will among the generations of divines that are growing up, these evidences will be brought to light, and the gradual development of modern Christianity from its original sources in the Wisdom-Religion will be historically traced.

All religions in their origin teach the divinity of man; but this teaching is afterwards hustled out of sight, and in its place we have a credal system supported by a hierarchy by which salvation is made conditional upon the acceptance of certain doctrines and conformity to certain requirements. It is of course inevitable and necessary that there should be organization, since every spirit must have an imbodiment of some kind. But the physical framework of a plant does not prevent it from growing and changing; and the outer form of religion must change from age to age to fit the growing need of the human spirit. And lastly, we must be willing to recognize the claims of other religions, most of them older than Christianity.

MANUALS IN THIS SERIES